Songs of Affirmation

The Key to Finding Your True Self Through the Power of Mantras

Dr. Jolene Church

Kortnee Thomas

ISBN: 978-0-578-34937-4

DEDICATION

Within each one of us is great power to call forth the knowledge that we seek. We are ever so grateful to serve as a conduit for the answer that you have pursued. We dedicate this book to the seekers. May you find the key to unlock your greatest desires.

CONTENTS

Introduction i

1 **Section I – The Foundation of Manifestation** 1

2 **Section II – Affirmation Categories (Alphabetical)** 13

Abundance

Accepting Criticism

Accountability

Anxiety/ Depression

Assertiveness

Becoming Focuses

Being More Mindful

Burnout

Career

Change

Clutter

Communication

Controlling Emotions

Courage

Dealing with Failure

Decision Making

Disappointment

Dream Big

Eating/ Food

Energy

Enjoying Life

Family

Financial

Finding your Passion

Forgiveness

Fresh Start

Friendship

Goal Achievement

Gratitude

Grief

Habits

Happiness

Helping Others

Honesty

Identifying your Strengths

Independence

Influence

Inner Peace

Innovation

Intuition

Loneliness

Love

Meditation

Mentoring

Negotiating

Perfectionism

Persistent

Play-it-safe

Procrastination

Relationships

Risk Taking

Self Esteem/ Self Confidence

Self-Growth

Self-Love

Sleep

Sexual

Stress

Taking Action

Teamwork

Time Management

Wealth

Wisdom

Working Smarter

3 **About the Authors** 378

INTRODUCTION

If you find yourself going around the same mountain, trudging along and not getting anywhere, your answer is right here. Transform your life and unlock your true power by redirecting and designing the vibrational energy around you.

Ancient people found the key to unlock the vastness of the universe as they tapped into the supernatural power of mantras. The alignment of neuroscience, ancient practices and sound are brought to life to bring about life changing transformation; manifesting the life, feelings and experiences that you desire.

Songs of Affirmation: The Key to Finding Your True Self through the Power of Mantras combines the universe-shifting power of affirmations with vibrational energy-changing song. If you desire greater peace and clarity, the mindfulness exercises and practices within these pages contain the ancient secret to get you there.

SECTION I

The Foundation of Manifestation

The Power of Sound

When you think about the word sound, what other word comes to mind? If are like most, the word is noise. For some, the answer is wind because of the sound of leaves rustling. Others may answer ocean with thoughts of waves crashing on the beach.

Sound by itself can seem rather nondescript, but combined with motion, more specifically, the energy of motion, the power of sound can more accurately be described, understood, and felt. Sound as noise can calm, as well as overwhelm our senses. The world around us can be chaotic and noisy.

External sound, what we can hear with our auditory senses, is only part of the sound and its energy associated with life. Internal sound, which derives from the subconscious mind, can become equally deafening as we 'hear' messages associated with fear, doubt, and limiting beliefs. The energy associated with our internal sounds influence the energy in motion of our external world. The louder the noise, the stronger the energy associated with that sound. Internal energy is transferred and manifested externally.

Indeed, life can be quite noisy, both outside and inside, but it's unfair to give noise a totally bad rap. Think of the noise created by the sound of laughter. It's healing and cathartic, both externally and internally. A smile can be 'contagious' and laughter 'warms the heart, yet in the practice of mindfulness, we are told that we must become 'still and quiet' to find peace. Sound is not the source of imbalance and calamity, just as noise isn't always negative. It's not the absence of sound that is where we find peace, peace is found by calming the energy put in action by sounds. True power is achieved by learning where the energy of sound is emitting, at what frequency, and how it's motion might be changed.

Sound is a powerful mechanism for transferring and exchanging energy, as sound is energy. The energy of sound is powerfully demonstrated through a sonic boom, which is created by the shock waves of a flying object exceeding the speed of sound. The energy boom becomes part of our energy as we sense through, most notably, our hearing. Although we can hear the sound, we also feel the energy associated with the sound. There are many examples in nature of the power of sound and the energy it exudes. Take for example, the alarming nature of an owl screeching or the thunder created by a majestic waterfall. Some sounds of nature, such as rain, waves, or the wind, are considered energizing and therapeutic as the energy of the sound becomes music to the ears and fuel for the soul.

Mankind has, since the beginning of time, created music through voice and instruments as a tool to soothe and heal the soul. Just think of a mother humming to her newborn infant to calm the child to sleep. Music is magical as it can transport us to another place in time. A melody can instantly captivate your heart, make your soul sing, and cause your feet to move. Just think about when an old song comes on the radio, in an instant you are transported back to that time. You remember where you were when you first hear the song and the memories associated with that time become awakened. The magical qualities of music stimulate energies in and around you, connecting people, times, memories, and feelings – all energies of all space and all time – this is the power of sound.

Ancient people combined scripture and song to create a powerful connection between the heavens and earth. These people learned how profound and impactful philosophical written words, amplified with the force of music, could touch the heart and illuminate the soul. They combined sacred writings or intent statements with melody, creating vibrational energy so as to reach higher levels of spiritual connectedness to one's true nature. Some of the earliest recorded illustrations of this are in ancient Vedic scriptures of Hinduism. These powerfully scripted *power sounds* are known as mantras and are the energetic equivalent of a sonic boom in the quantum realm.

Mantras are repetitive sounds that increase vibrational energy and penetrate our unconscious mind. The word *mantra* is derived from two Sanskrit words, *manas* (mind) and *tra* (tool). The literal translation is *mind tool.* From chants to symbolic sounds, mantras can be categorized into two groups, melodic and verse. For centuries, these powerful *mind tools* have been used in meditation to enable practitioners to reach an elevated level of spiritual connection, breaking the sound barrier and connecting into another realm – a realm of intentional manifestation.

"Mantra is a sound vibration through which we mindfully focus our thoughts, our feelings, and our highest intention," (Girish, 2016).

These tools of vibrational energy have a powerful effect on the world around us, as everything that we know is energy. Because everything exists in the field of quantum energy wherein the nature and behavior of all matter and energy is based on an atomic and subatomic level, as energy becomes more charged and vibrates faster, the matter around it changes. The vibrational energy from sound permeates the soul and has a profound effect on the body and the world as we know it. Focusing on the vibration energy during the mantra, enables us to quiet the chatter and background noise of life and welcome in intentional desire. Our energetic focus welcomes in the vibrational energy with what we desire instead of the energies going on in our consciousness and subconsciousness.

The most profound effect of the practice of mantras is that the environment of intentional energy is a catalyst for creation. We become creators as we choose the energy that is most suitable. Choosing our energetic focus enables us to shift away from what we do not want to experience and toward the experience that we desire. Change happens when we shift our focus and increase our vibrational energy toward what we desire.

Focused and intentional thought toward what you want is at the heart of manifestation. Manifestation within the *elevated state of being* serves as an incubator for desires to be birthed into the conscious realm. This is because the distracting and often blocking noise of the subconscious, which is also energy, is quieted and your intention becomes the focus of the dominant energy. The welcomed vibrational *noise* drowns out distracting background noise of what you would like to move away from. The most powerful manifestation sound devices for stimulating vibrational energy are affirmations. Affirmative words and phrases create an energetic connection within the quantum field to bring more of what you are grateful for.

Positive affirmations are powerful statements of gratitude and joy; they are based in abundance. Because not all energy vibrates at the same frequency, when we enter a higher vibrational frequency, we have the power to design and create our current and future experiences. Space and time do not exist in the quantum realm; they are one in the same. What you desire becomes part of the realm of creation in the quanta. In other words, what you think exists the moment you think it or dream it – good and bad. Because we continually have subconscious thoughts running in the background, like computer applications, focusing our energy on the experiences we desire helps us override any negative energy noise. Our focus on the energy of creation of what we desire while affirming what we are truly grateful and joyful for increases the waves of energy in the quanta toward us. Our dreams become closer as the waves become more rapid and closer and closer together. You may not hear the sound, but like waves crashing on the beach, you can feel the energy and you are moved.

The benefits of mantras go beyond elevated spirituality as the practice has been found to slow the breathing rate, reducing levels of physical stress, which contributes to additional physical ailments. The mental health benefits of mantras have caught the attention of neuroscientists who have been studying and quantifying the health benefits of this ancient practice. Scientists have found that while performing mantras, practitioners quiet the subconscious chatter and excessive negative noise going on in the background of the mind. This contributes to a calming, relaxed, and more focused state.

To better understand what it means to intentionally quiet chatter, envision a beehive that has been disrupted by an unwelcomed intruder, such as a bear. The hive, ordinarily buzzing in normal work activity is set into an alarmed state as the bear breaches the bees' realm. Our subconscious is similar to a disrupted hive as excessive chatter and noise create chaos. Our subconscious, like the violated hive becomes unsettled, disturbed and frenzied. The sound from the hive is alarming to passersby as the chaotic energy can not only be heard but also felt.

Conversely, an intentional state of quieting and refocusing of energy through the practice of mantras is like the energy resulting from a calming of the hive. Through intentional calming, threat is eliminated, chaos subsides, and the frantic buzzing quiets, transforming our subconscious back to a productive, energetic state. Quieted, one can still hear the buzzing of the bees, however, the chaotic energy slows. It is no longer unsettling, but instead peaceful, as the buzz from the hive unifies. The bees' energy becomes unified, focused, and once again productive.

Ripples on a Pond

All of what we know is a field of energy and possibility called the quanta. Oxford dictionary defines quanta as, "a discrete quantity of energy proportional in magnitude to the frequency in radiation it represents." To visualize the quantum field, picture a stone tossed into a still pond. The initial energy of the momentum of the stone flying supports the object being airborne. As the momentum wanes, the stone drops with a gravitational force, again momentum, into the water. Ripples begin to spread out in all directions from the spot that the energy of the stone broke through the surface of the water. The proportional magnitude to the frequency of radiation (vibration) expands and the ripples spread farther and farther. This is how our focused intention behaves as we put to use our powerful mind tool, the mantra.

Since primitive man, music has been an instrumental element of human existence. From voice to drums, from chants to melodies, music serves as a comforter, motivator, and a catalyst for spiritual connectedness. It is for this reason that when intention is aligned through melodic phrases that speak into creation desires of the heart, the universe unfolds its majesty like a red carpet. A world of your making awaits your calling it forth through melodic verses that sing to creation.

Chanting songs and verse, humming, drumming and singing all increase the energy in your space. Think of a song that moves you, a song that gets your feet tapping and you can hardly sit still. The energy inside of you is so motivated by the music that it vibrates you into action. The music becomes the stone thrown into the still pond and you become the waves. Your happiness and joyful energy vibrate through you and extend in waves out of you.

If you visualize a crowd at a concert, what do you see in your mind? Most likely, you see people standing and singing with smiling faces and waving arms. This is energy in motion as the music stimulates more and more energy throughout the crowd. The music is energy. The people are energy. Their thoughts as they interpret the song lyrics are energy.

Everything is energy and energy is everything. Energy always is and it never ends; it can only be transferred. Ancient people learned to tap into the power of the unseen, through something deep inside that they could feel, but couldn't explain. They learned that words of prayer and affirmation stirred the energy and miracles happened. They offered their prayers and affirmations as a song, repeating with intention, quieting the mind, and opening their hearts to the vibrational energy and they were transcended and elevated to another place; carried by the rippling waves.

How to Use This Book

This book is organized in a way to help you begin to practice the power of the mantra by providing you with a reference guide of affirmations arranged by topic. The intent of the content contained in the pages of this book is provided to help you get to a higher vibrational state. Through intentional energy shifting through the practice of affirmational mantras, what you desire becomes the energy that surrounds you. Because everything is energy and energy is everything, increasing your vibrational state increases the frequency that you transmit into the universe. What you desire already exists so increasing the energy around your intention helps the transfer of your desire come into your reality.

The book is organized, alphabetically by topic (e.g. love, abundance, peace, and success). The topical organization enables you to turn to the specific area that you would like to improve or focus on. If you desire focusing on love, turn directly to the section on love. There you will find affirmations to express as mantras that you can use to increase your vibrational energy to call forth love into your life.

Mantras are meant to be repeated in a melodic manner, again, they are a powerful combination of words that hold deep meaning and melody. There are no rules to how many repetitions or for any specific amount of time; you set the rules. You determine what feels right. The most important aspect is to choose the affirmation statements to chant as mantra(s) that feel right to you and repeat them every day, several times per day.

In selecting a topic, choose the one that calls to you. Begin by reading the words of the affirmation out loud. Read the verses several times. Again and again, read the words aloud that speak to you. Feel the vibration of the sounds as they cross your lips and touch your ears. Let the vibration ruminate. Feel the power of the words.

Next, sing the words. There is no right or wrong, and yes, you will very likely feel silly. That's okay. Sing. Add any musical tone such as a hum to the words as you read them. Your singing doesn't have to be in tune. It may help to just stretch out each word with a melodic note and then go up or down a note or octave for the next word. For example, an affirmation mantra might start out with, "I am living a blessed life." 'I' would be strung out for several seconds as, "I….y….y….y….y…..y…." Followed by, "a….m….m….m…." and so on. What's important is that you move from simply chanting words, to singing your words; this is where the true power comes from.

After stretching out each word, repeat the mantra by stringing together the words, "I…y… a…m…l…i…v…i…n…g…a…b…l…e…s…s…e…d…l…i …f…e…" Try ending on a higher note than the note that you started with.

Let's Get Started

As you get started, visualize yourself at a concert of your favorite musical artist. It's easy to understand the power within that environment to be moved by a song, guitar, drum, or a combination of all. The power unleashed within the crowd is found in the combined energy of the spoken word and musical tones. The energy that fill the souls of the concert goers is electric. This electricity is a feeling that you can achieve and maintain to invite in your desires through daily practice of mantras.

The affirmations on the proceeding pages are meant to be repeated and chanted. Chanting simply means that you will read the words as if it were a song. This becomes a mantra. The tune that you choose does not matter because the beautiful music from your soul cannot be wrong. My advice is to be kind to yourself. There is no room for judgement. Judgement ushers in the wrong energy.

Keep in mind, that judgement also has no place here, as mantras are used to quiet the chatter in your head by distracting the chaos of your mind. If you think of your mind like a computer, the background applications that run all the time bog down your computer's performance as they suck the energy away from the processor – in this case, your manifestation. To optimize performance, you will be turning off the background applications and focusing your processor on the task at hand, calming your mind and increasing your vibrational energy to connect to your core and third eye to call forth your desires. Let's get started.

The Basics

Bija (seed) mantras are used to clear the energy centers of the body, the chakras, or *wheels* in Sanskrit. This is a great starting place to introduce mantras into your daily routine. Bija mantras are simple, one-syllable sounds chanted in two syllables to increase the vibrational energy of the chakras as well as purify and cleanse them. These basic sounds can be used to prepare you for practicing ushering in intentional energies. We suggest, much like a singer does vocal exercises prior to performing that you practice humming, chanting, and singing the seven sounds below. It is our belief that these powerful seed sounds will act as a rooting device to your intentional mantras.

The table below provides the ancient seed sound for cleansing each of the seven (7) chakras.

Area	Chakra	Energy Point	Sound
Basic Trust	Muladhara	Root	LAM
Sexuality/Creativity	Svadhisthana	Sacral/Navel	VAM
Wisdom/Power	Manipura	Solar Pelux	RAM
Love/Healing	Anahata	Heart	YAM

Communication	Vishuddha	Throat	HAM
Awareness	Ajna	Third Eye	OM/AOM
Spirituality	Sahasrara	Crown	SO-HAM

SECTION II

Affirmation Categories

Abundance

I am an abundant creator.

I am the creator of my reality.

Opportunities bring prosperity.

I allow abundance to flow through me.

I am the Origin of every Path.

Abundance is all around me.

My superpower is attracting everything I need and desire.

I am grateful for everything that I have.

The universe is conspiring to make me -prosperous.

I let go of all resistance of lack, for I am abundance.

Abundance is my birthright.

The less I need, the more I have.

Accepting Criticism

Criticism is a teacher, I can either listen and learn or ignore and have to keep repeating the lesson.

I am thankful for all the criticism I receive, for it makes me stronger.

Being able to accept criticism without feeling hurt or offended is a milestone of inner progress and growth.

I receive criticism with an open mind, for true teachers tell you what you are doing incorrectly so that way you can grow.

Accountability

I am accountable for myself.

Each day I choose what to say, what to do, what choices I make, and how I react. I take responsibility.

My choices are mine to make.

I choose to embody the power that I am.

I cannot control every situation or circumstances, but I can control my reaction.

Affirmation

I am what I think.

I am a great creator.

I am grateful for the beauty I draw to me.

Anxiety/ Depression

Each day I have the ability to start new and today is a new day.

This will pass as I create a new experience.

The past is behind me and the future is creation from now. I choose to be in this present moment.

Even the darkest of days cannot hide forever from the sun.

Breathe, you are doing great.

Assertiveness

Saying “No” when you mean it is powerful.

I deserve respect.

I own who I am.

Becoming Focused

Being focused is a choice.

I am mindful in this *now moment.*

My energy will flow where I place my attention.

My potential is limitless, so I focus on where I place my energy.

Each task I complete is an accomplishment.

Being More Mindful

I am still in this place.

I choose to be present in this moment, taking in what is.

Now holds the power for all.

Being More Productive

I am creative and innovative in finding ways to do more.

I am the master of my time.

Productive energy is drawn to me.

I attract accomplishment.

Burnout

When I focus on what I desire, what I dislike fades away.

I choose my reality and my peace.

Better feelings are a thought away.

I am the creator of the life I desire.

Career

I am living my dream job.

What I desire, desires me too.

I am appreciated for all that I do.

When one door closes it's because a new path has opened, leading me to the door that was meant for me all along.

I am a vibrational match to what I seek.

My path is paved in gold.

Change

I welcome change.

I breathe in the new and breathe out what is ready to be let go.

The wind of change blows new opportunities into my reality.

I am releasing what is not in alignment so that what is can come through.

Change represents growth.

Charisma

Others are attracted to me.

My spirit is a magnet of kindness and joy.

People are drawn to the beauty of my energy.

Childhood

My past does not define me.

I am thankful for my experiences as they have prepared me for my purpose.

I am a cosmic child of the universe capable of anything.

I forgive and I am ready to heal.

I allow healing to flow through me.

I have the curiosity and excitement for life like a child.

I am worthy of love.

Clutter

My outside environment, which I can control, is an extension of my inner world.

Organization simplifies my reality.

I take the time to get my life in order.

I will start and finish today.

I feel more and more free the more I let go of what is no longer serving me.

Communication

I am a confident communicator.

Communication is a key to my success.

I am a highly effective communicator as I am a great listener.

I only say what I mean and mean everything that I say.

I am confident and this translates into my communication.

I am in touch with both what I say and do not say.

Controlling Emotions

Emotions are energy in motion.

My emotions are recognized, felt, and released.

I choose to focus on my reactions to others as my thoughts guide my feelings.

When I am triggered by my emotions, I choose to breathe and gain control of my thoughts so that I can choose a better feeling.

My energy chooses to flow to support my inner peace.

My feelings are valid. I honor each of my emotions that arise.

Courage

I am the master of myself.

I stand with pride for what I believe in.

I embrace each challenge with an open heart and mind.

I will do what I know is right in my heart, even if it feels wrong in my body.

I am courageous.

Dealing with Failure

When I get knocked down, I get back up.

When things fall apart, it is so other things can fall together.

Failure is defined by the thoughts I choose.

I choose to focus on what I have learned to better my future.

I am strong and resilient.

Perception creates my reality.

I rapidly turn perceived negatives into a positive new thought, shifting my reality.

Decision Making

I trust my decisions.

When decisions are difficult, I am able to trust the right path.

One wrong decision does not define my next decision.

The seeds I plant will grow.

Not making a decision is also a decision.

I clear all blockages that are impairing my decision making.

Disappointment

Darkness is temporary as I welcome in light to guide my path.

I take each set back as a rerouting, this is only the beginning of my journey.

Life is a learning process.

I will remain hopeful through disappointment, embracing where I am so that I will appreciate where I choose to be.

I use disappointment to strengthen my faith.

Dream Big

I am a big dreamer.

I am the creator of all I desire.

I envision my future with what I want.

I am the creator of my reality.

I make the rules for what I want to create.

I dream big because dreams do come true.

My dreams come true because I dream them.

Eating/Food

My body is an amazing energy producing machine.

I have a wonderfully effective metabolism.

I am nourished by the foods that I choose to feed my soul.

Food is energy and I choose good energy.

Energy

Everything is energy and energy is everything.

By realizing I am an energetic being I chose where I place my energy.

My energy is my superpower.

Negative energy is an inversion of positive energy.

Enjoying Life

I get great joy from life.

Joy chooses me daily.

I am living in my purpose.

I am designing the life I choose with every breath I take.

Family

I choose beauty in my relationships.

I love and appreciate my family.

Love is my greatest power.

Financial

I am living the lifestyle that I desire.

Money is attracted to me.

I love money and money loves me.

I attract abundance and wealth.

Wealth flows through me.

Money comes easily.

Finding Your Passion

My experiences are igniters of my passion.

My passion is powerful.

Passion burns within in me and ignites my future.

I am a beautifully passionate creator.

Forgiving

When I forgive others, I am expanding my heart.

Forgiveness is not always easy, but it is necessary.

I release all blockages around my heart and embrace a new beginning.

Forgiveness is the key to happiness.

Fresh Start

I am the beginning.

I am adaptable, resilient, and strong.

Today is the day I have dreamed of.

Friendship

People are attracted to my energy.

I enjoy my friends.

I attract friendships.

Goal Achievement

I take steps daily to achieve any goal I desire.

I am successful.

I am creative and able to find the path to what I choose to achieve.

Gratefulness

I have a grateful heart.

I am full of gratitude and joy.

My gratitude is a magnet for what I desire.

Grief

Through pain I can see love.

I allow the feelings of grief to flow through me along their path to peace.

Through grief can be found peace and love.

I appreciate and acknowledge the feelings of pain as I heal.

Habits

I have the power to create effective habits.

I am smart and creative and develop health habits that drive my success.

I am the power behind my positive habits.

Happiness

I am the designer of my happiness.

I am happiness.

Peace, love, and happiness are attracted to me.

Helping Others

Selflessness is an act of true love.

When I help others, I am planting a seed of kindness.

I am grateful to serve others.

Honesty

Others appreciate my honesty.

There is beauty in what is.

I am free to be me.

Identifying Your Strengths

My past experiences provide the building blocks for my growth.

I easily identify my strengths.

I am the great I am.

Independence

There is great beauty in my independence.

I am the only creator of my world.

My independence is my strength.

Influence

People listen to me.

The beauty and strength of my energy draws others to me.

I am respected.

Inner Peace

Inner peace is a state in which I choose.

Inner peace flows to and through me.

In this now moment, I am whole and complete.

I choose peace over worry.

Innovation

I am a creative being.

I am full of innovative ideas.

I attract innovation and creativity.

Intuition

My intuition is my internal guide.

I honor my inner knowing.

Intuition is the language of the body.

I trust my intuition.

My intuition protects me.

Loneliness

I am never truly alone.

Loneliness does not mean I need to settle.

I am whole. I am complete.

I know my worth.

I will attract relationships that are in alignment with my path.

Love

I am love.

Love is attracted to me and flows through me.

The power of love is of and about me.

Meditation

I am at peace with where I am.

I feel and listen to my breath, quieting the noise around me.

I am stillness. I am peace. I am what I desire.

Mentoring

I enjoy mentoring others.

As I teach and mentor others, I learn and grow.

Knowledge is power and sharing is caring.

Mindfulness

Being present in the now allows me to be in control of my reality.

I Am.

Thought is a powerful force that I choose to use wisely.

I am consciously making the best use of my Head, Heart, and Hands.

Negotiating

I am fair and trustworthy.

I am able to negotiate for results that bring harmony.

Agreement chooses me.

I get what I want as what I want is harmonious and peaceful.

Perfectionism

I am created in perfection.

I am the perfect creation of the universe.

Everything I design is perfectly designed.

Persistent

I push through.

My perseverance is my strength.

I am strong and persistent.

Giving up is not an option.

Play-it-Safe

I trust what I cannot see and believe that I can live the unseen.

Life is full of possibilities when we see it for its opportunities.

I choose to take the road less travelled and create my own path.

Procrastination

I choose to start now.

It all starts with the first step. I choose to take steps no matter the size.

Doing something always outperforms doing nothing.

Relationships

The time I devote to my relationships is priceless.

I choose to invest in those I care about.

I am the love that I give to others.

Risk Taking

There is no risk in believing in myself.

I will always take a chance on myself.

I am worth the risk.

Self-Esteem/Self-Confidence

I choose me.

I am enough.

I value my mind, body, and emotions.

I accept where I am at and that I am in control of where I am going.

Self-confidence fills me and is necessary.

I am a confident, beautiful being, living a life of purpose.

I am worthy.

Self-Growth

Growth and expansion is why I am here.

I am open to opportunities that allow me to grow.

I am committed to the steps I must take to reach my potential.

My mistakes do not define me, instead allow me to learn for personal growth.

Self-love

I am perfect, whole, and complete.

With each breath I take, I am more grounded and secure.

I am enough.

I am a divine creation of source, therefore I am complete.

I define myself.

In this now moment, I choose me.

I am Beautiful/ Handsome.

I am worthy of the love I desire.

Source created me through unconditional love, therefore I am love.

I am human. I'm allowed to mess up, but when I do I learn from my mistakes.

My current reality is not fixed, I have the ability to shift it.

This is my Now moment.

Sexual

I am comfortable with me.

I am a beautiful being capable of sexual expression.

My sexuality is an extension of my true self.

Simplifying Your Life

I allow simplicity into my life.

The less I focus on the materialism around me and more on my desires, the simpler life becomes.

I love just being me.

Sleep

I rest so that I can create.

Sleep allows my body and mind to heal.

I wake up feeling recharged, refreshed, and ready for the day.

Tomorrow is a new day; I rest so I can reset.

Speech Anxiety

I am becoming more confident as I speak to others.

Words and ideals flow easily to and through me.

Stress

Stress is an invitation to change my perspective.

I am relaxed and calm.

Breathe, I will get through this.

With each breath I release and let go of stress.

Taking Action

I take steps towards my goals daily.

I am in control of my life, and I do so through my actions.

My actions support my dreams.

I act on my inspirations.

Teamwork

There is great value in working with others.

Collaboration with others contributes to my success.

Others help me draw my dreams closer.

Time Management

I manage my time effectively.

Productivity is drawn to me.

I choose to manage myself which helps me to effectively manage time.

Wealth

I am wealth and abundance.

True wealth is peaceful and joyful; it is this truth I choose to live.

There is great wealth in love. I am love.

Wisdom

I welcome knowledge and experience to illuminate my path and increase my wisdom.

What I don't know, I am open to learn. What I have learned, I am willing to share.

I am the child of an infinitely wise universe; I am remembering.

Working Smarter

I am creative at finding new ways to get my work done.

I put in the work that gets things done.

Others admire how efficient I am at my work.

ABOUT THE AUTHORS

Dr. Jolene Church, ICF, PCC

Dr. Church is a California native, mother of four and grandmother. She and her husband, a trauma therapist, live in Northern California, where they enjoy riding their Harley Davidsons, spending time with family and friends, and living their best lives.

Dr. Church is a master life coach, change management expert, human resources professional and holds a Doctorate of Management in Organizational Leadership. Her work in cultural change and people optimization has helped transform and turn-around troubled businesses for corporate giants Citibank and Bank of America. Additionally, her work coaching executives of start-ups, non-profits, corporations, municipal governments, and religious and academic institutions (including USC Marshall School of Business) as well as providing life coaching to individuals has helped thousands of people become clear on how to achieve what they desire. Dr. Church uses her work in the areas of mindfulness and thought-redesign to help others manifest their dreams into reality - helping turn impossible into possible.

Kortnee Thomas

Kortnee is a mother of three and engaged to an amazing, supportive partner. They live in their nonnative, but new home state of Oklahoma. Curious by nature, this has led Kortnee to explore a wide variety of spirituality practices and modalities from Matras, Oracle & Tarot, Reiki, Energetic healing, Yoga,

Meditation, Quantum healing, and Crystal healing, to name a few.

Kortnee has always been intrigued with the way people think and how she might help them better control their mind. Majoring in Psychology, Kortnee set out to explore the correlation between the body and the mind; this opened the door to the fields of Neuroscience and Cognitive Behavior Therapy.

After experiencing a debilitating dark night of the soul, lasting for 3 years, Kortnee learned through experience how powerful the mind is and how perception creates one's reality. Through a year-long daily Mantra practice, Kortnee was able to rewire and create new circuits within her brain which ultimately shifted her reality. Taking back her power, she set out on a different course, one of self-healing.

In 2020 she opened a metaphysical crystal healing shop, Gemini Ascending, where through the power of crystals and personal intention, she could help people bring their energetic body back into alignment. Kortnee is currently developing a Quantum Reality Shift Healing Program where she takes her knowledge of the quantum and her personal healing experience and helps people remove blockages in their lives, then shifting to their desired reality.

www.ingramcontent.com/pod-product-compliance
Lightning Source LLC
LaVergne TN
LVHW020524100826
845148LV00010B/1329

* 9 7 8 0 5 7 8 3 4 9 3 7 4 *